EXPENSE LOG B

NAME ....

ADDRESS ....

PHONE ....

E-MAIL ....

Month:			Year:
Date:	Description Of Expense:	Payment Type:	Amount:

Total

notes

EXPENSES

DATE	EXPENSE TYPE	CATEGORY	METHOD	AMOUNT
			TOTAL:	

Month: | | | **Year:**

Date:	Description Of Expense:	Payment Type:	Amount:

Total

notes

EXPENSES

DATE	EXPENSE TYPE	CATEGORY	METHOD	AMOUNT
			TOTAL:	

Month:			Year:
Date:	Description Of Expense:	Payment Type:	Amount:
			Total

notes

EXPENSES

DATE	EXPENSE TYPE	CATEGORY	METHOD	AMOUNT
			TOTAL:	

Month:			Year:
Date:	Description Of Expense:	Payment Type:	Amount:

Total

notes

EXPENSES

DATE	EXPENSE TYPE	CATEGORY	METHOD	AMOUNT
			TOTAL:	

Month:			Year:
Date:	Description Of Expense:	Payment Type:	Amount:
			Total

notes

EXPENSES

DATE	EXPENSE TYPE	CATEGORY	METHOD	AMOUNT
			TOTAL:	

Month: Year:

Date:	Description Of Expense:	Payment Type:	Amount:
			Total

notes

EXPENSES

DATE	EXPENSE TYPE	CATEGORY	METHOD	AMOUNT
			TOTAL:	

Month:			Year:
Date:	Description Of Expense:	Payment Type:	Amount:
			Total

notes

EXPENSES

DATE	EXPENSE TYPE	CATEGORY	METHOD	AMOUNT
			TOTAL:	

Month:			Year:
Date:	**Description Of Expense:**	**Payment Type:**	**Amount:**
			Total

notes

EXPENSES

DATE	EXPENSE TYPE	CATEGORY	METHOD	AMOUNT
			TOTAL:	

Month:			Year:
Date:	Description Of Expense:	Payment Type:	Amount:
			Total

notes

EXPENSES

DATE	EXPENSE TYPE	CATEGORY	METHOD	AMOUNT
			TOTAL:	

Month:

Year:

Date:	Description Of Expense:	Payment Type:	Amount:

Total

notes

EXPENSES

DATE	EXPENSE TYPE	CATEGORY	METHOD	AMOUNT
			TOTAL:	

Month:			Year:
Date:	Description Of Expense:	Payment Type:	Amount:

Total

notes

EXPENSES

DATE	EXPENSE TYPE	CATEGORY	METHOD	AMOUNT
			TOTAL:	

Month:

Year:

Date:	Description Of Expense:	Payment Type:	Amount:

Total

notes

EXPENSES

DATE	EXPENSE TYPE	CATEGORY	METHOD	AMOUNT
			TOTAL:	

Month:			Year:
Date:	Description Of Expense:	Payment Type:	Amount:

Total

notes

EXPENSES

DATE	EXPENSE TYPE	CATEGORY	METHOD	AMOUNT
			TOTAL:	

Month: **Year:**

Date:	Description Of Expense:	Payment Type:	Amount:

Total

notes

EXPENSES

DATE	EXPENSE TYPE	CATEGORY	METHOD	AMOUNT
			TOTAL:	

Month: | | | **Year:**

Date:	Description Of Expense:	Payment Type:	Amount:

Total

notes

EXPENSES

DATE	EXPENSE TYPE	CATEGORY	METHOD	AMOUNT
			TOTAL:	

Month:			Year:
Date:	Description Of Expense:	Payment Type:	Amount:
			Total

notes

EXPENSES

DATE	EXPENSE TYPE	CATEGORY	METHOD	AMOUNT
			TOTAL:	

Month:			Year:
Date:	Description Of Expense:	Payment Type:	Amount:
		Total	

notes

EXPENSES

DATE	EXPENSE TYPE	CATEGORY	METHOD	AMOUNT
			TOTAL:	

Month:

Year:

Date:	Description Of Expense:	Payment Type:	Amount:

Total

notes

EXPENSES

DATE	EXPENSE TYPE	CATEGORY	METHOD	AMOUNT
			TOTAL:	

Month: **Year:**

Date:	Description Of Expense:	Payment Type:	Amount:

Total

notes

EXPENSES

DATE	EXPENSE TYPE	CATEGORY	METHOD	AMOUNT
			TOTAL:	

Month:			Year:
Date:	**Description Of Expense:**	**Payment Type:**	**Amount:**
			Total

notes

EXPENSES

DATE	EXPENSE TYPE	CATEGORY	METHOD	AMOUNT
				TOTAL:

Month:			Year:
Date:	Description Of Expense:	Payment Type:	Amount:
		Total	

notes

EXPENSES

DATE	EXPENSE TYPE	CATEGORY	METHOD	AMOUNT
			TOTAL:	

Month:			Year:
Date:	**Description Of Expense:**	**Payment Type:**	**Amount:**
			Total

notes

EXPENSES

DATE	EXPENSE TYPE	CATEGORY	METHOD	AMOUNT
			TOTAL:	

Month:			Year:
Date:	Description Of Expense:	Payment Type:	Amount:
			Total

notes

EXPENSES

DATE	EXPENSE TYPE	CATEGORY	METHOD	AMOUNT
			TOTAL:	

Month:			Year:
Date:	Description Of Expense:	Payment Type:	Amount:
			Total

notes

EXPENSES

DATE	EXPENSE TYPE	CATEGORY	METHOD	AMOUNT
			TOTAL:	

Month:			Year:
Date:	Description Of Expense:	Payment Type:	Amount:

Total

notes

EXPENSES

DATE	EXPENSE TYPE	CATEGORY	METHOD	AMOUNT
			TOTAL:	

Month:

Year:

Date:	Description Of Expense:	Payment Type:	Amount:
			Total

notes

EXPENSES

DATE	EXPENSE TYPE	CATEGORY	METHOD	AMOUNT
			TOTAL:	

Month:

Year:

Date:	Description Of Expense:	Payment Type:	Amount:

Total

notes

EXPENSES

DATE	EXPENSE TYPE	CATEGORY	METHOD	AMOUNT
			TOTAL:	

Month:

Year:

Date:	Description Of Expense:	Payment Type:	Amount:

Total

notes

EXPENSES

DATE	EXPENSE TYPE	CATEGORY	METHOD	AMOUNT
			TOTAL:	

Month:

Year:

Date:	Description Of Expense:	Payment Type:	Amount:

Total

notes

EXPENSES

DATE	EXPENSE TYPE	CATEGORY	METHOD	AMOUNT
			TOTAL:	

Month:			Year:
Date:	Description Of Expense:	Payment Type:	Amount:
			Total

notes

EXPENSES

DATE	EXPENSE TYPE	CATEGORY	METHOD	AMOUNT
			TOTAL:	

Month: | **Year:**

Date:	Description Of Expense:	Payment Type:	Amount:

Total

notes

EXPENSES

DATE	EXPENSE TYPE	CATEGORY	METHOD	AMOUNT
			TOTAL:	

Month:

Year:

Date:	Description Of Expense:	Payment Type:	Amount:

Total

notes

EXPENSES

DATE	EXPENSE TYPE	CATEGORY	METHOD	AMOUNT
			TOTAL:	

Month:			Year:
Date:	**Description Of Expense:**	**Payment Type:**	**Amount:**
		Total	

notes

EXPENSES

DATE	EXPENSE TYPE	CATEGORY	METHOD	AMOUNT
			TOTAL:	

Month:

Year:

Date:	Description Of Expense:	Payment Type:	Amount:

Total

notes

EXPENSES

DATE	EXPENSE TYPE	CATEGORY	METHOD	AMOUNT
			TOTAL:	

Month:			Year:
Date:	Description Of Expense:	Payment Type:	Amount:
			Total

notes

EXPENSES

DATE	EXPENSE TYPE	CATEGORY	METHOD	AMOUNT
			TOTAL:	

Month:

Year:

Date:	Description Of Expense:	Payment Type:	Amount:

Total

notes

EXPENSES

DATE	EXPENSE TYPE	CATEGORY	METHOD	AMOUNT
			TOTAL:	

Month:

Year:

Date:	Description Of Expense:	Payment Type:	Amount:

Total

notes

EXPENSES

DATE	EXPENSE TYPE	CATEGORY	METHOD	AMOUNT
				TOTAL:

Month:			Year:
Date:	**Description Of Expense:**	**Payment Type:**	**Amount:**
		Total	

notes

EXPENSES

DATE	EXPENSE TYPE	CATEGORY	METHOD	AMOUNT
			TOTAL:	

Month:			Year:
Date:	Description Of Expense:	Payment Type:	Amount:
			Total

notes

EXPENSES

DATE	EXPENSE TYPE	CATEGORY	METHOD	AMOUNT
			TOTAL:	

Month:				Year:
Date:		Description Of Expense:	Payment Type:	Amount:
				Total

notes

EXPENSES

DATE	EXPENSE TYPE	CATEGORY	METHOD	AMOUNT
			TOTAL:	

Month: Year:

Date:	Description Of Expense:	Payment Type:	Amount:

Total

notes

EXPENSES

DATE	EXPENSE TYPE	CATEGORY	METHOD	AMOUNT
			TOTAL:	

Month: | **Year:**

Date:	Description Of Expense:	Payment Type:	Amount:

Total

notes

EXPENSES

DATE	EXPENSE TYPE	CATEGORY	METHOD	AMOUNT
				TOTAL:

Month:

Year:

Date:	Description Of Expense:	Payment Type:	Amount:

Total

notes

EXPENSES

DATE	EXPENSE TYPE	CATEGORY	METHOD	AMOUNT
			TOTAL:	

Month:			Year:
Date:	Description Of Expense:	Payment Type:	Amount:

Total

notes

EXPENSES

DATE	EXPENSE TYPE	CATEGORY	METHOD	AMOUNT
				TOTAL:

Month:

Year:

Date:	Description Of Expense:	Payment Type:	Amount:

Total

notes

EXPENSES

DATE	EXPENSE TYPE	CATEGORY	METHOD	AMOUNT
			TOTAL:	

Month:			Year:
Date:	**Description Of Expense:**	**Payment Type:**	**Amount:**
		Total	

notes

EXPENSES

DATE	EXPENSE TYPE	CATEGORY	METHOD	AMOUNT
			TOTAL:	

Month:			Year:
Date:	**Description Of Expense:**	**Payment Type:**	**Amount:**
			Total

notes

EXPENSES

DATE	EXPENSE TYPE	CATEGORY	METHOD	AMOUNT
			TOTAL:	

Month:			Year:
Date:	Description Of Expense:	Payment Type:	Amount:
		Total	

notes

EXPENSES

DATE	EXPENSE TYPE	CATEGORY	METHOD	AMOUNT
			TOTAL:	

Month:

Year:

Date:	Description Of Expense:	Payment Type:	Amount:

Total

notes

EXPENSES

DATE	EXPENSE TYPE	CATEGORY	METHOD	AMOUNT
				TOTAL:

Month:			Year:
Date:	Description Of Expense:	Payment Type:	Amount:

Total

notes

EXPENSES

DATE	EXPENSE TYPE	CATEGORY	METHOD	AMOUNT
			TOTAL:	

Month:			Year:
Date:	Description Of Expense:	Payment Type:	Amount:

Total

notes

EXPENSES

DATE	EXPENSE TYPE	CATEGORY	METHOD	AMOUNT
			TOTAL:	

Month: | | | **Year:**

Date:	Description Of Expense:	Payment Type:	Amount:
		Total	

notes

EXPENSES

DATE	EXPENSE TYPE	CATEGORY	METHOD	AMOUNT
			TOTAL:	

Month:

Year:

Date:	Description Of Expense:	Payment Type:	Amount:

Total

notes

EXPENSES

DATE	EXPENSE TYPE	CATEGORY	METHOD	AMOUNT
			TOTAL:	

Month: | | | **Year:**

Date:	Description Of Expense:	Payment Type:	Amount:

Total

notes

EXPENSES

DATE	EXPENSE TYPE	CATEGORY	METHOD	AMOUNT
			TOTAL:	

Personal Expense Tracker

Month:			Year:

Date:	Description Of Expense:	Payment Type:	Amount: